Valuing Yourself

by

Marna Owen

GLOBE FEARON

Pearson Learning Group

Project Editors: Helene Avraham, Laura Baselice, Lynn W. Kloss
Executive Editor: Joan Carrafiello
Production Manager: Penny Gibson
Production Editor: Nicole Cypher
Marketing Manager: Marjorie Curson
Interior Electronic Design: Patricia Smythe
Illustrator: Donna Nettis
Photo and Art Coordinator: Jenifer Hixson
Electronic Page Production: Eric Dawson
Cover Design: Eric Dawson
Cover Photograph: © Steve and Mary Beran Skjold

Reviewers:

Dorie L. Knaub, B.A., M.S.
Special Education Specialist
Downey Unified School District
Downey, California

Odalis Veronica Martin, B.A., M.S.
Special Education Teacher
Dade County Public Schools
Miami, Florida

Photo Credits: **p. 4**: © Melanie Carr, Zephyr Pictures; **p. 8**: Mahon Photographic Illustrators; **p. 14**: © 1994 Jeffrey High, Image Productions; **p. 31**: © Richard B. Levine; **p. 53**: © Steve and Mary Beran Skjold; **p. 59**: © Kathy Sloane, Photo Researchers.

ISBN 0-8359-1260-4
Printed in the United States of America
8 9 10 11 12   07 06 05

1-800-321-3106
www.pearsonlearning.com

Contents

Chapter 1

What is Self-Esteem?

Chapter Objectives

- Recognize high self-esteem.
- List three reasons for working on self-esteem.
- Explain how to change self-esteem.

Words to Know

self-esteem: an opinion of oneself
value: to regard or think of highly
self-respect: opinion of one's own character and
   actions
self-confidence: a sureness or trust in oneself

Something About Her

Meet Jane. Her favorite subjects in school are art, music, and math. She gets good grades in those classes. She doesn't do as well in other classes, like English and science. Jane has to work extra hard in those classes.

People say that Jane's best feature is her hair. It is long, thick, and wavy. Like most teenagers, Jane has trouble with her skin.

Jane lives with her mother and little brother. Her parents split up when she was 12. She sees her father on some weekends and holidays. But, it's not as often as she would like.

There is one thing about Jane that is not so average. People who meet her for the first time say there is something special about her. It's something they wish they had, even though they can't name it.

➤ **What Do You Think?**

Take a guess at what makes Jane special.

What is Self-Esteem?

Jane has something called high self-esteem. **Self-esteem** is your opinion about yourself. People with high self-esteem think quite well of themselves. They **value** who they are and what they are able to do.

"Oh," you might say. "I know somebody who is really stuck up. He thinks he is better than everyone else. Does he have high self-esteem?"

No. People with high self-esteem respect the rights, feelings, and actions of others. They see the value in the opinions of others. People who ignore the value in others' opinions lack high self-esteem.

How do you recognize a person with high self-esteem? People with high self-esteem have **self-respect.** They like themselves and are comfortable with who they are. Jane knows she is good at some things and not so good at others. She accepts this about herself. She believes she has the right to be happy. She knows she deserves a good life even if she isn't good at everything she does.

People with high self-esteem also have **self-confidence.** They are able to handle challenges and problems. They take control of their lives. When they fail, they forgive themselves and try again.

High self-esteem is *not* about having money or being famous. Those things can make you feel better for a while. But the feeling doesn't always last. Self-esteem comes from inside you. It is about how much you value yourself, no matter who you are, or what you have.

Self-esteem comes from inside you. It is not what others think of you. It's what you think of yourself.

➤ Check Your Understanding

Put a check (✓) next to the items below that help you recognize a person with high self-esteem.

1.   How rich the person is

2.   How good-looking the person is

3.   How willing the person is to solve problems

4.   How many friends the person has

5.   How famous the person is

6.   How much self-respect the person has

7.   How much the person respects the rights of others

8.   How well the person does in school

➤ Write About It

Think about someone you know who has high self-esteem. Write three things that the person has said or done that shows high self-esteem.

_____

_____

_____

➤ Try This

Stand in front of a mirror. Pretend you are having a "low self-esteem day." Now, pretend you are having a "high self-esteem day" and look again. Did your looks change? How?

_____

Why Work on Self-Esteem?

Self-esteem is something that every person has. With high self-esteem you can reach more of your goals. If your goal is to make a lot of money, high self-esteem can help you. If your goal is to live a simple life, high self-esteem can help you, too.

Self-esteem helps you get along with others. When you respect others, they usually return the respect. If problems do arise, high self-esteem can help you solve them. When Jane is hurt by a friend, she tells the person how she feels. She tries to work out the problem by talking about her feelings. She faces the problem. She believes in her ability to work things out.

High self-esteem can help you live a healthy life. People with high self-esteem take care of their bodies. They accept the fact that they are not perfect. They forgive themselves for their

Facing problems is never easy, but self-esteem can help.

flaws. They recognize their positive traits. Jane makes a point of doing something special with her hair every morning. It makes her feel good and look confident, even when the rest of her looks a bit raggedy!

High self-esteem is not a cure-all. People with high self-esteem can feel lonely, sad, and angry. Bad things happen to them, just as they happen to everyone else. But people with high self-esteem tend to handle these problems in healthy ways.

➤ If You Could Put It in a Can...

Imagine that you have found a way to package high self-esteem. In the space below, design an advertisement for your new product. What would you call it? What can it do? How much would it cost? How would you advertise it? What would the container look like? Put all this information in the ad.

➤ Think About It

Can you think of anything that is more valuable than high self-esteem? Explain your answer in the space provided.

_____

_____

How Can You Change Your Self-Esteem?

What kinds of situations can hurt a person's self-esteem?

There was a time that Jane's self-esteem was not very high. During that time, nothing seemed to go right. Jane often found herself fighting with her friends. She snapped at her mother. She felt angry and sad being around her father. Her grades in school dropped. She began to cut classes. Things seemed to grow worse with each passing day.

One of Jane's teachers saw the change and took time to talk to her. Jane was feeling badly about her parents' divorce. She felt it was her fault. She desperately wanted her parents to get back together.

"Jane," her teacher said, "you don't have much control over your parents. But you do have some control over your own life. You do not have to let this get you down. It's your choice."

Jane suddenly did not feel so powerless. Little by little, she began to change.

Like Jane, you have the power to change your self-esteem. Here is what it takes:

1. Look at who you are and how you feel about yourself. Think about why you feel this way.
2. Believe you have control over how much you value yourself.
3. Change how you think and act.

Changing your self-esteem is not easy. It takes commitment and practice. This book will give you some ideas on how to make a change. But wanting to change has to come from you!

➤ Getting Started on Self-Esteem

List two endings under each phrase to complete the sentence.

I feel good about myself when . . .

_____

_____

I don't feel good about myself when . . .

_____

_____

If I could change anything about myself, I would . . .

_____

_____

The things I like most about myself are . . .

_____

_____

I feel self-confident when . . .

_____

_____

I feel worried when . . .

_____

_____

Chapter Summary

- Self-esteem is your opinion about yourself. People with high self-esteem respect the rights, feelings, and actions of others. They have self-respect and are self-confident.
- People with high self-esteem are able to work toward their goals. They tend to get along well with others. They handle their problems in a healthy, positive way.
- To change your self-esteem, you must look at who you are and how you feel about yourself. You must identify why you feel this way. You must believe you have control over how much you value yourself. You must begin to change how you think and act.

Chapter Review

Words to Know

Using complete sentences, write a definition of self-esteem.

_____

_____

Recognizing Self-Esteem

Decide what level of self-esteem is shown in each situation below. Write the words "high self-esteem" or "low self-esteem" in the space provided.

1. A person fights every time someone disagrees with him or her.

_____

2. A person always listens to the other side of a story.

_____

3. A person tries to make a lot of money so that others will like him or her.

_____

4. A person chooses a job because it is something that he or she enjoys.

_____

Getting Personal

Why is it important to have high self-esteem?

_____

_____

Chapter 2

Finding Out Who You Are

Chapter Objectives

- Explain the relationship between knowing who you are and self-esteem.
- Define rules to live by.
- Identify values and goals.

Words to Know

advice: an opinion or suggestion
ability: the quality of being able to do something
goal: an aim or purpose
moral code: rules having to do with right and wrong
religion: a system of beliefs or worship

Be True to Yourself

It was graduation day at the high school. Students and their families sat in the noisy gym. Several people spoke. First, the school principal addressed the crowd. The class president spoke next. Then, a young man in a wheelchair took the stage. The crowd became quiet.

"My name is Joe Myers," the student said. "Most of you know me. In my first year of high school, I had an accident that changed my life. It took away the use of my legs. For a long time, I did not care about myself. I had no dreams. I could barely decide what to wear each morning."

"Then one day I watched a race on TV. In the race were people like me, people in wheelchairs. Afterwards, one of the racers spoke. He talked about the importance of living each day with a purpose."

"I began to think about who I was. What did I believe? What was important to me? What did I want out of life? Today I feel alive and strong. I am so glad to be graduating with you! I am here to offer you some **advice.** Think carefully about who you are and what you want to be. This is the first step to success."

Who You Are and Self-Esteem

Joe values who he is. He has high self-esteem. One of the ways he built his self-esteem was by figuring out who he was and what he wanted to be. Here is what Joe did:

What do you value most?

- He thought about what he believed to be right and wrong. Among other things, Joe decided it was wrong to waste his life. He decided it was right to live with a purpose.
- He decided what his values were. He identified what was important to him. At one time, Joe valued his **ability** to walk more than anything. This changed after the accident. He could no longer do certain things. Joe realized that he still had the abilities to think, act, and work with others. He began to value these abilities more than walking.
- He set **goals,** or aims and purposes, for himself. Joe decided he wanted to educate people about what it's like to be disabled. He became active in a group that works for the rights of the disabled. Joe hopes to run for public office someday.
- Joe's accident forced him to figure out who the "new Joe" was. Figuring out who you are and what you want to be is important for all teenagers. During this time, you change from a child into an adult. You no longer do things just because others tell you to. You do things because you are responsible enough to make your own choices. If the choices you make help you to respect yourself and the rights of others, your self-esteem will grow.

➤ Drawing Relationships

Follow the steps below.

1. Write the word "values" on one of the lines.
2. Write the word "goals" on one of the lines.
3. Write "rules to live by" on one of the lines.
4. Draw an arrow from each of the lines to the words "high self-esteem."
5. High self-esteem can help you live by your rules and values. It can also help you achieve your goals. To show these relationships, draw an arrow from "high self-esteem" to each of the lines.
6. Show your drawing to a classmate. Explain what the drawing means in your own life.

_____   _____

HIGH SELF-ESTEEM

_____

Choosing Rules to Live By

The first step in figuring out who you are is to decide what is right and what is wrong. Rules for right and wrong are sometimes called a **moral code.**

Your moral code is a very personal matter. You should spend some time thinking about it. Your parents, friends, and laws, must all be considered. You must also think about your religion, or system of beliefs or worship. In addition, you must think about your rights, and the rights of others.

➤ Think About It

Put a "1" next to the factor that you think is most important to consider when deciding what is right or wrong. Identify the next most important factor with a "2" and so on.

_____ Laws   _____ Friend's beliefs

_____ Family's beliefs   _____ Your religion

Begin to write your moral code by completing the sentences below. Your code should respect your rights and the rights of others.

1. Caring for My Body

It is right to _____

It is wrong to _____

2. How I Treat My Friends

It is right to _____

It is wrong to _____

3. How I Treat Strangers

It is right to _____

It is wrong to _____

4. How I Treat Animals

It is right to _____

It is wrong to _____

5. When I'm Angry

It is right to _____

It is wrong to _____

6. When I Know Others are Breaking the Law

It is right to _____

It is wrong to _____

Values and Self-Esteem

Another way to build your self-esteem is to know—and live by—your values. Values can help you make choices when things are not simply a matter of right or wrong.

One Thursday night, Joe faced this decision. Should he take his girlfriend out or should he stay home and study? Joe thought about his values. He really wanted to graduate from high school. He was not doing well in a certain class. He needed to spend more time studying.

Joe realized he valued graduating more than having a good time. He decided to stay home. Joe felt good about his decision. He had thought about his values and honored them. His self-esteem grew.

Your values change throughout your life. At one time, you may value wearing the latest clothes. At another time, where you live may be very important to you. As you grow older, you will value the kind of work you do. When you are faced with choices, it is always good to stop and ask, **"What is more important to me? How will my choice affect how I feel about myself?"**

How have your values changed?

➤ Thinking About Values

Below is a list of values. Circle the five values that are **most important** to you.

Blending in	Dressing fashionably	Being popular
Making money	Doing well in school	Taking risks
Being a leader	Being kind	Having fun

➤ Self-Esteem Builder

Use your values to help you decide what to do in each of the following situations.

1. You are not doing well in math. There is a big test tomorrow. Your best friend wants you to come over to watch a great movie.

What do you decide to do?

_____

Do you feel good about your decision? Explain why.

_____

_____

2. The drama coach wants you to try out for the school play. She thinks you could be a star. You are not entirely comfortable speaking before a large group.

What do you decide to do?

_____

Do you feel good about your decision?

_____

_____

3. You have been invited to a party hosted by a person you really like. The party is on the same night that you begin a new job.

What do you decide to do?

_____

Do you feel good about your decision?

_____

_____

Goals and Self-Esteem

Goals are an important way to express who you are and what you want. Goals are the things you want to achieve. Graduating from high school could be a goal. Getting along with your family could be a goal. Becoming an electrician could be a career goal. Having high self-esteem could even be a goal.

Goals that help your self-esteem grow are goals that fit your values. Not everyone can be a famous sports star. Goals should make you stretch, but still be within your reach. Your goal may be to marry, have children, and be a good parent. Or, your goal may be to get any job that will allow you to rent an apartment and buy a CD player. What you value, and who you are, determine your goals.

Goals and self-esteem work together. When you know what your goals are, and you work toward them, your self-esteem grows. In turn, your self-esteem helps you to achieve your goals. It keeps you moving forward and on track. If you stumble or fail, your self-esteem helps you try again.

In the coming chapters of this book, you will learn more about how to achieve your goals. For now, start to build your self-esteem by deciding what your goals are.

Setting achievable goals can raise your self-esteem.

➤ Personal Goals

Think about the five values you identified as being important to you. Write a personal goal that fits these values.

_____

_____

➤ Self-Esteem Builder

Complete the sentences below. Check the lines that are true.

1. In school, my goal is to _____

This goal:

_____ Fits my values.

_____ Is something I can really do.

_____ Is something worth doing.

2. For work, my goal is to _____

This goal:

_____ Fits my values.

_____ Is something I can really do.

_____ Is something worth doing.

3. With my family, my goal is to _____

This goal:

_____ Fits my values.

_____ Is something I can really do.

_____ Is something worth doing.

4. With my friends, my goal is to _____

This goal:

_____ Fits my values.

_____ Is something I can really do.

_____ Is something worth doing.

Chapter Summary

- You can help your self-esteem grow by having a clear picture of who you are. High self-esteem can help you be true to who you are. Knowing yourself means having rules to live by, a set of values, and goals.

- Rules for right and wrong are sometimes called a moral code. A person's moral code is a personal matter. Family beliefs, your friends, your religion, and laws all help you decide upon a moral code.

- Values are the things that are important to you. Goals are the things you want to achieve. The goals you choose should fit with your values.

Chapter Review

Words to Know

Match each word on the left to its meaning on the right. Write the correct letter in the space provided.

_____ **1.** advice

_____ **2.** ability

_____ **3.** goal

_____ **4.** moral code

_____ **5.** religion

a. a system of beliefs or worship

b. an aim or purpose

c. the quality of being able to do something

d. rules having to do with right and wrong

e. an opinion or suggestion

Self-Esteem Builders

Complete each sentence with one of the following words.

moral code　　　　**goal**　　　　**values**

1. "I won't do that," John told his friend. "That is wrong." John's _____ is helping him make decisions and build his self-esteem.

2. "Listen to me," said Sara's father. "You're going to work for me. That's all there is to it."

   "No, Dad. You don't understand. There is something more important to me," replied Sara. Sara is talking to her father about her _____. They help her make decisions that are right for her and build her self-esteem.

3. "I finally decided to get help with my homework," said Jill. "I really want to pass this class." Jill has decided to set, and work toward, a _____. This will help her self-esteem.

Chapter 3

Being Positive

Chapter Objectives

- Explain how being positive affects self-esteem.
- Identify personal strengths and weaknesses.
- Use strengths and weaknesses in positive ways to build self-esteem.

Words to Know

positive: helpful and constructive
trait: a feature or quality that helps set something or
    someone apart from others

How Did She Do That?

Parker was watching a new girl at the dance. She sat near the wall. Yet, you couldn't call her a loner. She looked great!

Parker introduced himself to her. Her name was Keri. She gave him a big smile. Parker asked her to dance.

"I'm not a very good dancer," she smiled.

Parker decided to give up. He thought Keri did not like him. He started to turn away, but she called him back.

"I'm not scared of talking," she said to him. "How about sitting down for a minute. Maybe if I get to know you, I'll find the courage to dance."

Parker and Keri talked and laughed. At the end of the evening, they still had not danced.

"Still scared?" asked Parker.

"A little," answered Keri.

Parker shrugged his shoulders. "This is strange," he said. "You keep telling me you are afraid to dance. Yet, after getting to know you, I think of you as confident."

> ## ➤ What Do You Think?

How could Keri be both confident and afraid?

Being Positive and Self-Esteem

Keri is presenting herself as a **positive** person. She is putting her best side forward.

"Well," you might say, "Keri says she is a bad dancer. She says she is afraid. What is so positive about that?"

Keri has a positive attitude about herself. She has learned to accept who she is. She admits that dancing is her weakness. She shows off her smile, looks, and personality which are her strengths.

Keri is positive in another way. She faces her feelings and controls them instead of letting them control her. By doing these things, Keri is more confident about herself. How she looks and what she says sends a positive message to the people she meets.

This chapter explores several ways to become more positive. Being positive will help your self-esteem grow.

➤ **Check Your Understanding**

If the statement is true, circle "T." If the statement is false, circle "F."

People with high self esteem . . .

1. are good at everything.   T   F

2. are never afraid.   T   F

3. accept their feelings.   T   F

4. focus on their strengths.   T   F

5. are good dancers.   T   F

Believing in Your Worth

Keri was not always confident. In the past, she had been told that she was clumsy. Kids laughed at her in gym class. She was always the last to be picked for a team sport. The more Keri listened to others, the worse she got. Soon she began to believe she couldn't do anything right. She didn't trust herself at anything. She became shy and unhappy.

One day Keri's older brother took her aside. "You know, you should quit listening to what everybody else tells you. Take a look in the mirror. So what if you're clumsy? You are still a worthwhile person. Don't let anybody tell you otherwise."

Keri followed her brother's advice. She took a long look in the mirror. She stayed perfectly still. She saw an attractive girl with sleek black hair and big brown eyes. Keri started to do some dance moves. "Boy, I really am clumsy," she thought. Her heart sank.

Keri sat down and made a list of her traits. **Traits** are features or qualities that set one person apart from others. She thought about more than her outside appearance. She looked inside herself.

Keri listed both her strengths and weaknesses. She saw herself as a kind person with a sense of humor. These were strengths. She saw not standing up for herself as a weakness.

Keri looked at the list. She decided to accept who she was, even if she didn't like all her traits. That was her first step to being positive. Already, her self-esteem was starting to grow.

How do you think Keri could raise her self-esteem?

➤ Self-Esteem Builder

1. Make a list of traits you like about yourself (or your strengths), and traits you do not like (or weaknesses). Be sure to list equal numbers of strengths and weaknesses. In making the list, think about:

   • what you are interested in
   • what you can do
   • what you would like to be able to do
   • things you've achieved since you were born
   • what you'd like to do in the future
   • your appearance
   • what you like about yourself
   • what you do not like about yourself

<table>
<tr><td align="center">Strengths</td><td align="center">Weaknesses</td></tr>
<tr><td>_____</td><td>_____</td></tr>
<tr><td>_____</td><td>_____</td></tr>
<tr><td>_____</td><td>_____</td></tr>
<tr><td>_____</td><td>_____</td></tr>
<tr><td>_____</td><td>_____</td></tr>
<tr><td>_____</td><td>_____</td></tr>
<tr><td>_____</td><td>_____</td></tr>
<tr><td>_____</td><td>_____</td></tr>
</table>

2. Look at the list. Say to yourself, "I accept all of these things about myself. Even with my weaknesses, I am still a worthwhile person." Believe it!

Making the Most of Your Strengths

Keri decided to "show off" her strengths more. When she got up in the morning, she did two things. She identified one of her strengths. Then she thought about how she could use that strength during her day.

What exactly did she do? She laughed more to show off her smile and sense of humor. Since she loved to read, she began to work in a reading program for young children. These things helped Keri build her self-confidence and self-esteem.

Learning to make the most of your strengths is a good way to build your self-esteem. If you are good at art, hang up your artwork in your room. If you are a kind person, volunteer your time with people less fortunate than yourself. By doing so, you will not only "show off" your strengths. The practice will cause these positive traits to become even stronger!

Imagine a friend comes to you for help. He has made a list of his strengths. But he can't think of ways to "show them off." Suggest a way your friend could showcase each of the following traits.

1. I have a good singing voice.

_____

_____

2. I can draw well.

_____

_____

3. I can make people laugh.

_____

_____

4. I like to work hard.

_____

_____

> ## Self-Esteem Builder

Look back at your list of strengths. Choose one. Describe how you have already "shown off" this strength. Then name another way of showcasing it.

_____

_____

Turning Weaknesses into Strengths

You may ask, "Should I just accept my weaknesses?" Not at all! However, you must be realistic about the things you can change. You must use your values and goals to decide what *you* really want to change.

Keri did not ignore her weaknesses. She thought about them a lot. She asked herself, "Do I really want and need to change these things?"

To help her decide, Keri thought about her values and goals. She wanted to become a teacher someday. Keri realized that being clumsy would not keep her from reaching that goal. Suddenly, being clumsy did not seem very important. While others were on playing fields, she could do something she really enjoyed—like reading.

You can do the same thing. Take time to look at your weaknesses. Are some of your weaknesses really strengths in disguise? Which traits actually get in the way of your goals? Which are important for you to change?

Sometimes, you don't need to change.

> ## ➤ Strengths in Disguise

Listed below are two traits that could be called weaknesses. Name one positive thing that could come out of each trait.

1. Being short

_____

2. Talking too much

_____

Risking Positive Change

Keri learned to accept her clumsiness. Even though she accepted her shyness, she decided it was something she wanted to change. Shyness could get in the way of her goals. Keri wanted to be able to say what she felt. She wanted to stand up for herself. This was important to her.

Keri identified speaking up for herself as a personal goal. When she wanted to speak up, but couldn't, she thought about her feelings. She realized she was afraid. She noticed how her body would tense up. She felt her throat tighten. She found it hard to think clearly.

Keri compared her feelings of fear to what she felt like when relaxed. She took deep breaths. She loosened her shoulders. Keri began to focus on relaxing each time she felt scared.

Keri practiced relaxing and speaking up in familiar places. At the dinner table, she talked more with her family. She raised her hand more in class. Sometimes, she would feel embarrassed after hearing herself speak. But she told herself, "I'm getting better each time." Little by little, speaking up seemed to get easier.

One day in gym, some girls began to make fun of Keri. Even though she felt scared, she looked them in the eye. "I know I'm clumsy," she said. "But you'll just have to live with it like I do. Now let's get on with the game." After a while, the girls stopped teasing her. They began to accept who she was.

Deciding to change is one thing. Working to change something about yourself is another.

How do you feel when you risk making a change?

It means having a good plan and working hard. It means risking that you might fail. It means forgiving yourself when you fail and moving on.

Is it worth the effort? Yes! Changing a weakness will make you more comfortable with who you are. It will help your self-esteem grow!

➤ Self-Esteem Builder

1. Look back at your list of strengths and weaknesses. Ask yourself, "Which of these traits is most important for me to change? Which will stop me from reaching my goals?" Write this trait on the line below.

_____

2. Rewrite one of your weaknesses as a positive goal. Remember, the goal should be something you are able to do and is worth achieving. Here are two examples to help you.

Weakness	Goal
Not good at math	Get a "C" in math class
Fight too much	Control my anger

_____

_____

3. Identify three things you could do to achieve your goal.

_____

_____

_____

Chapter Summary

- Being positive is an important way to build self-esteem. You can be positive about who you are and what you feel.
- Every person has different traits. Regardless of your traits, you are a worthwhile individual. You deserve respect and have the ability to respect others.
- You can use your traits to build your self-esteem. You can use your values and goals to decide what you need to change about yourself. You can take steps to make the change happen.

Chapter Review

Words to Know

Using complete sentences, explain each term in your own words.

1. positive _____

_____

2. trait _____

_____

Self-Esteem Builders

If the statement is true, circle "T." If the statement is false, circle "F."

1. People with lots of weaknesses are not worthwhile.   **T**   **F**
2. Accepting your strengths and weaknesses can help build your self-esteem.   **T**   **F**
3. Being positive means never being angry or afraid.   **T**   **F**
4. Facing your feelings is one way to be positive.   **T**   **F**
5. Values and goals help people decide what they want to change about themselves.   **T**   **F**

Getting Personal

What is the main thing that keeps you from being positive? What is something you could do to overcome this obstacle?

_____

_____

Chapter 4

Belonging

Chapter Objectives

- Explain the relationship between belonging and self-esteem.
- List three steps to help find positive ways of belonging.
- Practice making responsible choices when under pressure from friends.

Words to Know

community: any group that lives in the same place or
   has common interests

peer pressure: power used by friends to influence
   another's actions or thoughts

Feeling the Need

James was moping around the house one
day. His sister looked at him.

"What's wrong with you?" she asked.

"I don't know," said James. " It seems that
all I do is try to stay out of trouble."

"You mean try to stay out of gangs," replied
his sister.

James nodded. "What does it get me? I
come home. I do my homework. I watch
television. I go to bed. Some life!"

"So, you'd rather be getting into trouble?"
asked his sister.

"No. I don't want trouble," snapped James.
"I just feel like I need to be part of something.
Something bigger than myself. Do you know
what I mean?"

James's sister gave him a hug. "You are part
of this family," she reminded him.

"Yes," he said, "but, it just isn't enough."

➤ **What Do You Think?**

What is causing James to feel this way? _____

_____

How Do We Meet the Need to Belong?

Human beings are social creatures. This means that people need and like to be around others. Part of what James is feeling is the need to be with friends. He also feels the need to be part of something bigger than himself. He wants to feel part of a community.

A **community** is any group of people that lives in the same place or has common interests. Your family, your school, and your group of friends are all types of communities. Being part of a community is an important building block of self-esteem. As part of a community, you feel safer. If the community is working toward goals you agree with, you feel more confident. If you belong to a positive community, your self-esteem will grow.

Teenagers often feel the need to belong. As a child, your most important community was your family. As a teenager, you begin to branch out and look for a new community. Finding a positive community can be a challenge.

➤ How Does It Feel?

Try this exercise with your classmates.

1. Walk back and forth in front of the class with two classmates.

2. Then walk back and forth in front of the class by yourself.

3. Which time did you feel more confident? Why? _____

_____

_____

Finding Positive Ways to Belong

James began to think about his need to belong. He decided to join a group. He wasn't very athletic, so sports were out!

One day, James saw an ad in the school newspaper. "Come join the newspaper staff," it said. "We need people with good ideas who will work hard. The next meeting is Thursday at 3:30 PM in Room B-2."

James liked the school newspaper. He wasn't a good writer, but he liked to work hard. He decided to go to the meeting.

James did not know anyone at the meeting. Yet he stayed and listened to the editor. She explained all the jobs involved in creating the paper. James found this very interesting. Then she asked for volunteers to work in teams to cover stories. James decided to join the staff.

What groups or clubs does your school offer that interest you?

At first, James felt very nervous about joining. Little by little, he learned to be part of his team. He learned how to find information. His writing skills improved. When his team's first story appeared in the paper, he was proud of himself. He felt like he was finally part of something important. His self-esteem grew!

➤ **What Do You Think?**

What did James risk by joining the paper? What did he stand to gain?

_____

_____

Finding a Positive Community

The following steps can help you find a positive community.

1. Think about your rules for living, your values, and your goals. Use these as a guide for finding a positive community.
2. Learn about groups in your area. Church, school, and volunteer organizations are a good place to start. Ask your librarian to help you locate groups that do things you like to do.
3. Visit groups that interest you. Keep an open mind. Going to one meeting does NOT mean you have to join! Talk to members of the group.
4. If you cannot find a group that interests you, start one of your own. Put up fliers to find others who might want to join you.

Self-Esteem Builder

1. Look at the lists below. Check the items that match your interests, goals, or values. You may even add your own items to each list.

Sports

___ baseball

___ basketball

___ dance

_____

Concerns

___ equal rights

___ safer streets

___ cleaner environment

_____

Work/Study Skills

___ math

___ writing

___ computer skills

_____

Hobbies

___ computer games

___ music

___ fashion

_____

2. Write three ways you could find a group with the same interests.

_____

_____

_____

3. Write the name of a group that you think you want to join. Explain.

_____

_____

A Test of Wills

Where could you learn about groups in your community?

Except for the school newspaper, James made a point of keeping to himself. He didn't want any trouble. One day, trouble came looking for him.

It was his old friend, Henry. Henry and James had been best friends in grade school. When they reached high school, Henry joined a neighborhood gang. The gang was known for breaking the law.

"You should join us," said Henry. "We have everyone's respect. People stay out of our way. We stick by each other. We protect each other. It's a great feeling, James."

James knew what was coming next.

"We want you to join us," said Henry. "We need you."

James never wanted to join the gang. He had no interest in breaking the law or ending up in jail. But he knew that if he didn't join, Henry would be angry.

James had to stop and think. He had to make a difficult decision. Most importantly, he had to be able to live with his choice.

➤ What Do You Think?

What should James do? How will his decision affect his self-esteem?

_____

_____

_____

Being Responsible for Your Choices

James is facing **peer pressure** from Henry. Peer pressure can be the power friends have to influence you to think or act a certain way. Peer pressure is a powerful force. You want your friends to like you. You want to be part of their community.

Peer pressure can be positive or negative. Suppose Henry had been trying to get James to raise money for homeless people. This peer pressure would be positive. Unfortunately, peer pressure is often negative. The peer pressure James feels to join the gang is an example of negative peer pressure. This type of peer pressure is one reason why people may use drugs and commit crimes.

Peer pressure is a part of life. What should you do when you face it? Remember that you are responsible for your choices. Say to yourself:

- I am responsible for my own choices.
- I am the one who must live with my choices.
- My choices should stand for who I am as a person.
- To make good choices, I should think about my values, goals, and moral code.

It may be hard to think or act in a way that is different from your friends. Try to explain your point of view to them. Good friends will listen and accept your choice. Sometimes, you will just have to say, "No thanks," and walk away. In the end, your friends will respect you more. You will respect yourself and your self-esteem will grow.

What's the hardest thing about standing up to your peers?

➤ Self-Esteem Builder

In the following situations, you have to make a choice.

1. Lately you've been feeling lonely. Your friends offer you some drugs to make you feel better. "Come on," they say. "Let's have a good time."

   a. Who is responsible for making this choice?

   _____

   b. Who has to live with this choice?

   _____

   c. Which choice fits your moral code, values, and goals?

   _____

   d. Which choice is better for your self-esteem?

   _____

2. Your friends invite you to "have some fun" tonight. They plan to spray paint on the side of the school.

   a. Who is responsible for making this choice?

   _____

   b. Who has to live with this choice?

   _____

   c. Which choice fits your moral code, values, and goals?

   _____

   d. Which choice is better for your self-esteem?

   _____

➤ Self-Esteem Builder

Read the situation below. Follow the steps to role-play, or act out, the situation with some classmates.

Ciro's friends want him to join their soccer team. Ciro has never played soccer. He feels that he'd rather spend his free time doing something he enjoys. His friends won't take no for an answer. They continue to pressure him.

1. Think of at least three different ways Ciro could handle this situation.

2. Role-play, or act out, each choice listed. Assign the part of Ciro to one classmate. The other students should take the role of Ciro's friends.

3. Take a vote to determine which way of handling the situation is best for Ciro. Predict how this choice would affect Ciro's self-esteem.

Chapter Summary

- All people share the need to belong. One way you meet that need is by joining a group or community with common interests or goals. Belonging to a positive community is an important building block to self-esteem.

- You belong to communities with friends and families. Finding other groups or communities can help build self-esteem. This is especially important for teenagers. There are many things you can do to find a group to join. Think about your interests and goals. Research groups in your area. Explore them with an open mind. Look for groups that deal with things that interest you. Be confident that the group will appreciate having you as a member.

- The need to belong makes peer pressure a powerful force. Negative peer pressure can harm your self-esteem. Even with peer pressure, you are responsible for your own choices. Your choices should always fit your moral code, values, and goals. Standing up to peer pressure can be hard. But, in the long run, it is good for your self-esteem.

Chapter Review

Words to Know

Using complete sentences, explain each term in your own words.

1. community

_____

2. peer pressure

_____

Self-Esteem Builder

Pretend that a neighbor comes to you with a problem. His friends want him to steal some sports equipment from the school. He doesn't believe stealing is right. His friends say he must do this in order to remain part of their group. What advice would you give your neighbor?

_____

_____

_____

Getting Personal

Think about a situation in which you faced peer pressure. Was the peer pressure positive or negative? What did you do? Would you do the same thing today? Write your answers on the lines below.

_____

_____

_____

Chapter 5

More Ways to Build Self-Esteem

Chapter Objectives

- Understand that building and maintaining self-esteem is a lifelong process.
- Explain the relationship between health and self-esteem.
- List three ways to build self-esteem in others.

Words to Know

counselor: a person who gives advice

role model: a person who is respected and imitated by others

compliment: an expression of praise or respect

Work to Keep It

Julia found herself at the Youth Center. Her **counselor,** or advisor, Marta, came out to talk to her.

"What's wrong?" Marta asked.

"I don't know," said Julia. "Last year, I felt pretty good about myself. I had things under control. Now I feel as if I'm sliding backward."

"What do you mean?" asked Marta.

"Well, my mom is drinking again. I failed one of my classes. I feel ugly. What's happening to me? Why can't I be like you?"

"Like me?" Marta said surprised.

"Yes. You always seem to be so together. I guess you have something I don't."

Marta shook her head. "Don't kid yourself, Julia. It's true that some of us get more breaks in life than others. But feeling good about yourself can be hard work, no matter who you are. Self-esteem is like having your dream car. When it's new and shiny, you feel great. Then life's little accidents start to nick the paint here and there. Maybe you even get in a major crash. Most of the time, you can find ways to repair your car. It's the same with repairing your self-esteem. It takes time and energy and hard work."

Julia trusted Marta. "OK," she said. "Then let's get to work."

➤ Self-Esteem Review

Once you build your self-esteem, you must work to keep it up. This is what Julia needs to do. Circle the items below that Marta might have shared with Julia about self-esteem.

1. Your self-esteem is your responsibility.

2. Have a set of rules that help you know what is right and wrong.

3. Always do what your friends want you to do.

4. Don't focus on your values and goals.

5. When you feel sad, lonely, or angry, hide your feelings.

6. When you feel sad, lonely, or angry, face your feelings.

7. Think about your weaknesses as much as possible.

8. Show off your strengths.

9. When you make a mistake, blame yourself and feel bad.

10. When you make a mistake, accept responsibility for it. Then find positive ways to recover.

11. When your friends pressure you, be responsible for your choices.

12. Join communities and groups that share your interests and goals.

13. Have realistic goals that make you stretch.

14. Break your goals into small steps. Complete the steps one at a time.

15. Choose to work on weaknesses that may get in the way of your goals.

How We Look and Feel

One of the things Julia told Marta was that she felt ugly. Her feelings about her looks were affecting her self-esteem.

How you look and feel is an important part of self-esteem. When your self-esteem is low, it is easy to stop taking care of yourself. When your self-esteem is high, you look and feel better.

Marta told Julia that when the rest of her life improved, she would look and feel better. In the meantime, Julia could change how she looked and felt. Here is the advice Marta gave:

How do your feelings affect your self-esteem?

- Exercise a little every day. Even 10 minutes of stretching will help you feel better. Longer periods of more active exercise will also help you when you feel lonely, angry, or sad. By working out such feelings through exercise, you are more able to cope with the feelings in healthy ways.

- Send positive messages about your looks. Stand tall. Walk with your shoulders back and your chin up. Smile more. Be proud of yourself!
- Begin the day by waking up and thinking of something positive. A positive attitude will help you look and feel good.
- Remember to focus on your strengths. We all have things about our looks that we like and don't like. Nobody is perfect! Even fashion models use makeup, clothing, and lighting to make the most of their strengths.

Julia tried following these guidelines. She began by walking 20 minutes every day. She felt more in control. She lost some weight and felt better about her appearance. Once again, Julia's self-esteem started to grow.

➤ Think About It

1. Write four words that describe how you feel after exercising.

_____   _____

_____   _____

2. Review your list. Did you identify more positive or negative feelings?

_____

3. What value have you placed on exercise in the past? Have your feelings about the value of exercise changed after reading about Julia?

_____

_____

➤ Self-Esteem Builder

Rate yourself from 1 to 5 in the following areas. Circle the number that best describes you.

A. I look and feel good.

1	2	3	4	5
Never	Sometimes	Regularly	Almost Always	Always

B. I exercise to look better.

1	2	3	4	5
Never		Regularly		Always

C. I exercise to feel better.

1	2	3	4	5
Never		Regularly		Always

D. I send positive messages about how I look and feel by the way I stand, sit, and walk.

1	2	3	4	5
Never		Regularly		Always

E. I smile as often as possible.

1	2	3	4	5
Never		Regularly		Always

F. I think about something positive in the morning.

1	2	3	4	5
Never		Regularly		Always

G. I try to show off my positive features.

1	2	3	4	5
Never		Regularly		Always

Identify two areas where you circled a 3 or below on the preceding page.

_____

_____

Think about the first area. What are some things you could do to improve that rating?

_____

_____

Think about the second area. What are some things you could do to improve that rating?

_____

_____

Predict the effect these changes would have on your self-esteem.

_____

_____

_____

Building Self-Esteem in Others

Julia worked hard on how she was feeling. She began to face her anger about her mother's drinking problem. She joined a group for teenagers whose parents abused drugs. She focused on her goals and began to work harder in school.

One day, Julia went to thank Marta. Marta had a surprise for her.

"We want you to come work at the Youth Center," said Marta. "We think you would be good at sharing what you've learned with others."

Julia took the challenge. She found that, as she helped others, her own self-esteem grew.

Helping others is another important way to build your own self-esteem. You do not have to work in a Youth Center or be a counselor. Here are some easy things you could do:

- Remember you are a **role model.** As a role model, others look up to you and imitate you. Due to your age, you are a role model to younger children. Keep this in mind as you go about your everyday business. Act in a way that shows respect for yourself and others. When others imitate you, their self-esteem will grow.

  Who looks up to you?

- Learn to give compliments. **Compliments** are comments that show praise or respect. Compliments should always be honest. Try to make them as specific as possible. Instead of saying "You look nice today," say, "I really like what you're wearing today. It shows off the color of your eyes." You'll feel good and so will the person you are complimenting.
- Take time to listen to others. Keep an open mind. By respecting others' opinions, you can help their self-esteem grow. At the same time, you will earn their respect.

➤ Self-Esteem Builder

Complete this exercise with two partners. Your partners may be family members, friends, or classmates.

1. Look at your partners. Think of 3 compliments you could give to each of them right now. Be sure they are honest statements. Write the compliments below.

   _____

   _____

   _____

   _____

   _____

   _____

2. Say at least two of the compliments to your partners.

3. Explain how you felt when saying the compliments to your partners.

   _____

   _____

   _____

4. How do you think your compliments made your partners feel?

   _____

   _____

5. Think of two other things you could do to build self-esteem in others. Write your ideas below.

   _____

   _____

Chapter Summary

- Building and maintaining self-esteem is a lifelong process. To keep your self-esteem high, you must take responsibility for how you feel. You must work actively to cope with life's challenges.
- How you look and feel can affect your self-esteem. Three ways to look and feel better are to exercise regularly, give positive messages by how you stand, sit, and walk, and to make the most of your strengths.
- Building self-esteem in others is an important way to maintain your own self-esteem. Three ways to do this are to be an active role model, to give compliments to others, and to take the time to listen to others.

Chapter Review

Words to Know

Match each word on the left to its meaning on the right. Write the correct letter in the space provided.

_____ **1.** compliment   **a.** person who is imitated by others

_____ **2.** counselor   **b.** an expression of praise and respect

_____ **3.** role model   **c.** a person who gives advice

Building Self-Esteem

Suppose a friend comes to you with a problem. He doesn't like the way he looks. He wishes he could change his entire face. He feels like he just doesn't have the energy to do anything. Identify three pieces of advice you would give your friend.

_____

_____

_____

Getting Personal

Think about the people in your life. Whom do you look up to as a role model? Explain why you admire this person.

_____

_____

_____

_____

_____

Valuing Yourself

Words to Know

Match each word on the left to its meaning on the right. Write the correct letter in the space provided.

_____ **1.** ability		**a.**	an opinion of oneself
_____ **2.** advice		**b.**	to regard or think of highly
_____ **3.** community		**c.**	opinion of one's own character and actions
_____ **4.** compliment			
_____ **5.** counselor		**d.**	a sureness or trust in oneself
_____ **6.** goal		**e.**	an opinion or suggestion
_____ **7.** moral code		**f.**	the quality of being ablew to do something
_____ **8.** peer pressure		**g.**	an aim or purpose
_____ **9.** positive		**h.**	rules having to do with right and wrong
_____ **10.** religion		**i.**	a system of beliefs or worship
_____ **11.** role model		**j.**	helpful and constructive
_____ **12.** self-confidence		**k.**	a feature or quality that helps set something or someone apart from others
_____ **13.** self-esteem			
_____ **14.** self-respect		**l.**	any group that lives in the same place or has common interests
_____ **15.** trait			
_____ **16.** value		**m.**	power used by friends to influence another's actions or thoughts
		n.	a person who gives advice
		o.	a person who is respected and imitated by others
		p.	an expression of praise or respect

About Valuing Yourself

Answer each question in the space provided.

1. What steps can you take to improve your self-esteem?

   _____

   _____

2. How do values affect self-esteem?

   _____

   _____

3. Why is it important to make choices based on your moral code, values, and goals?

   _____

   _____

Getting Personal

Take a few minutes to review the chapters in this book. Think about what you have read. Identify the three most important things you have learned from this book.

1. _____

2. _____

3. _____

How will you use what you have learned from this book in your everyday life?

   _____

   _____

Glossary

ability: the quality of being able to do something, 16

advice: an opinion or suggestion, 15

community: any group that lives in the same place or has common interests, 40

compliment: an expression of praise or respect, 57

counselor: a person who gives advice, 51

goal: an aim or purpose, 16

moral code: rules having to do with right and wrong, 17

peer pressure: power used by friends to influence another's actions or thoughts, 45

positive: helpful and constructive, 28

religion: a system of beliefs or worship, 17

role model: a person who is respected and imitated by others, 57

self-confidence: a sureness or trust in oneself, 6

self-esteem: an opinion of oneself, 6

self-respect: opinion of one's own character and actions, 6

trait: a feature or quality that helps set something or someone apart from others, 29

value: to regard or think of highly, 6